Contents

Enjoying spelling	5
Homonyms	6
Homophones (1)	7
Homophones (2)	8
How to use a dictionary	9
Mnemonics	10
Plurals	
words which end in -y	11
- s or es?	12
oddities	13
collective nouns	14
Prefixes (1)	15
pre, post; inter, trans, over;	
uni, multi	
Prefixes (2)	16
un, dis, de; re;	
prefixes as words	
Prefixes (3)	17
ad; com, con, co	
Prefixes (4)	18
sub super	
Proof reading	19
Roots	20
parts; whole words	
Sounds and their spelling:	
eigh or *aigh?*	21
igh (1))	22
igh (2)	23
ough (as in *rough)*	24
ough (as in *through)*	25
ough (as in *though)*	26
ough (as in *cough* & as in *Slough)*	27
ough (as in *borough)*	28
ough or *augh?*	29

Sounds and their	
The *sh* sound	30
The *ur* sound (1)	31
The *ur* sound (2)	32
The *ur* sound (3)	33
The *ur* sound (4)	34
would / could / should (1)	35
would / could / should (2)	36
Suffixes (1)	37
consonant + y; silent e	
Suffixes (2)	38
ly; ish; ese, an	
Suffixes (3)	39
making verbs into nouns & nouns	
into verbs (or, er, ion, ment, ing)	
Suffixes (4)	40
to double or not to double	
Syllables	41
Using apostrophes	42
Vowel sounds and their spellings	43
What is English?	44
What's in your name?	45
What's in your address?	46
Terms used in *Spelling Worksheets*	47
Useful reference books	48

If you would like to receive our catalogue of publications for teaching reading, spelling and basic maths., please write to or telephone the publishers at this address:

Brown and Brown,
Keeper's Cottage,
Westward,
Wigton,
Cumbria
CA7 8NQ
Tel. 016973 42915

Enjoying spelling

People communicate mainly with words. Human language probably began as a series of sounds which were gradually formed into words. People only started writing words down when they settled to live in one place and needed to organise themselve as a community. In Britain, there was no standard system of spelling words until about 200 years ago, when the first real dictionary was published. Until then, people spelled as they liked. Nowadays, things have gone to the other extreme and our jobs and livelihoods can depend on the way we spell; and we rely on dictionaries to help us.

There is no doubt that it is easier for everyone to understand each other if there is a basic system of spelling to use, but learning to spell should be a pleasure, not a chore. It is important to remember that language is a living thing and people change it to suit their own needs. Every day, hundreds of new words come in and old words fall out of use or change their meaning. Looking at words and where they come from, the way they are spelt and how they link up with each other is fascinating.

These days, there are words everywhere - on the streets, in shops, on advertising hoardings - not just in books and newspapers and magazines. We take in many spellings simply by seeing them every day and the more we look the easier and more interesting it can become.

Words and writing will always be with us. Learning to be a good speller is not easy, but enjoying it is half the battle.

A   Where did you last see these?

Say where you think you last saw each of these everyday words:

Car Park	Menswear	through	Babycare	Hardware
the	Spares	Carlsberg	Department	Road

B   Parts

1.   *Make a list of words which contain the same spelling pattern and sound as those underlined below.*

   SP**AR**   B**oo**ts   Moth**er**c**are**   **Ll**oyd's   Abbey Nation**al**

2.   a.   *Many of the names of cars end in a vowel (**e.g.** Clio, Mini, Corsa). What do you think is the reason for this? How many more can you think of?*

   b.   *Make a list of other products or companies whose name ends with a vowel (**e.g.** Asda, Martini, Bisto)*

Words within words

How many words can you find in

MARKS AND SPENCER

without changing the order of the letters.

How many words?

How many words of 2 or more letters can you make from

SUPERMARKET

using the letters in any order you like.

Homonyms

Homonym from Greek: *homonumos* - of the same name (*homos* - same + *onoma* - name)
Homonyms are words which have the same spelling but have different meanings.
Sometimes homonyms are pronounced differently; sometimes they sound the same.

e.g.   a row (*argument*)   a row (of *peas* or *seats* or *houses*)
         to row (*a boat*)   to row (*to argue*)

A   What is the other meaning?

*Each of the words in **bold** in this piece can mean something different. Put each word into a sentence which shows its other meaning.*

It was a **fine** day in **spring** when the jockeys lined up for the first **race** at Newmarket. It was the start of the **flat** racing season and there was a big crowd in the **stand**. To be first past the **post** today would mean a large cheque for the young rider on *All Mine* and a chance to **train** at the best stables in the country. It was a first-rate **field** and just one **slip** could cost him a **place**, but that was all **part** of the excitement which no jockey would **miss**.

B   Identical twins?

These pairs of words look the same, but if they are pronounced differently they have different meanings. Say each word aloud, then put it in a sentence which explains its meaning.

1.	lead	lead	**3.** tears	tears
2.	sow	sow	**4.** reading	Reading

C   What do they mean?

The answers to the clues below are homonyms. Think of the word which fits each pair of clues.

1. **a.**   The back of a boat

   b.   Strict; humourless

2. **a.**   The front of a boat

   b.   Bend over from the waist

3. **a.**   Humorous (*Ha! Ha!*)

   b.   Odd (*peculiar*)

4. **a.**   Event with stalls and sideshows

   b.   Light-coloured hair

   c.   Just; correct; equal

5. **a.**   Clothes or equipment

   b.   Part of a car which helps it to change speed

Homophones (1)

Homophone Word origin: Greek *homos* - same, + *phone* - sound, voice.

Homophones are words which sound the same but are spelt differently and have different meanings (*e.g.* **been** and **bean**).

- ☐ There are a lot of homophones in English mainly because there have been many changes in the way that vowel sounds are written down and the way that they are spoken over hundreds of years.

- ☐ A good way to cope with homophones is to learn each word and its spelling in the context you would normally use it, so that you remember what it means, how it sounds and how it looks, all together.

- ☐ It is useful to keep a check list of the most common ways of spelling each vowel sound.

- ☐ There are exercises on homophones throughout *Spelling Worksheets*, but this sheet covers some commonly confused spellings of vowel sounds.

A What's wrong?

There are 15 homophones in this piece which have been used wrongly. Can you spot them and give the correct spelling?

Bill's site wasn't very good, so he had to where glasses all the time. He was always having accidents. He had been off work for a weak after bumping into a lamp post and braking his glasses. He had a severe pane in his chest and he could only sea with one eye.

One evening, he thought he wood take a bus into town to meat his friend for a pint. As he got to the mane road, the bus was just moving off. He jumped aboard and paid his fair. He was halfway up too the top deck when the driver jammed his brakes on. Bill fell backwards down the stares and broke his leg.

"It seams I'm always in the wrong plaice at the wrong time," he tolled the doctor in Casualty.

B How do you spell it?

*All these words have a long **a** sound in them. Put the right word in each gap.*

1. Most _____ pop stars get a lot of fan _____ from teenage girls.
   (*male / mail*)

2. The man spent his _____ money on a large _____ and chips.
   (*steak / stake*)

3. It poured with _____ on the day when the Champion Jockey ended his long _____ and held the _____ of his favourite horse for the last time.
   (*rein / rain / reign*)

4. To make a _____ pizza you need to _____ plenty of cheese on top.
   (*grate / great*)

5. In days gone by, tea was _____ for visitors by a _____ . (*made / maid*)

Homophones (2)

> **Homophone** Word origin: Greek *homos* - same, + *phone* - sound, voice.
>
> Homophones are words which sound the same but are spelt differently and have different meanings (*e.g.* **been** and **bean**).
>
> ❐ There are a lot of homophones in English mainly because there have been many changes in the way that vowel sounds are written down and the way that they are spoken over hundreds of years.
>
> ❐ A good way to cope with homophones is to learn each word and its spelling in the context you would normally use it, so that you remember what it means, how it sounds and how it looks, all together.
>
> ❐ It is useful to keep a check list of the most common ways of spelling each vowel sound.
>
> ❐ There are exercises on homophones throughout *Spelling Worksheets*, but this sheet covers some commonly confused spellings of vowel sounds.

A Jokes

Homophones are often used in jokes. Pick out the homophones in these jokes and newspaper items. Write down the other spelling of the homophone if it is not already given.

1. **Customer**   Waiter, what sort of soup is this?

    Waiter   It's bean soup, sir.

    Customer   I don't care what it's been. What is it now?

2. My parents are in the Iron and Steel trade. My mother irons and my father steals!

3. **DOVER ROAD** Semi-detached house with sea through lounge.

    (Folkestone, Hythe & District Herald)

4. It has been discovered that Wales is sinking into the sea because it has too many leeks in the ground.

5. **FOR SALE: KIELDER FERRIES**

    A family-run Ferry & Cruise business. This highly profitable business has soul ferrying rights on Kielder Water, one of Northumberland's largest tourist attractions.

    (Newcastle Journal)

B What's the difference?

These sound the same but what's the difference between them? Put each in a sentence which shows the difference in meaning.

1.	apart	a part	4.	already	all ready
2.	about	a bout	5.	altogether	all together
3.	around	a round	6.	away	a way

WRITING   *Write down a joke that you know, then underline any words in it which are homophones. Put each homophone into a sentence to show its meaning.*

How to use a dictionary

Dictionaries are the best guides to good spelling. Any skilled worker will say how important it is to have the right tools for the job. Dictionaries are the tools everyone needs to help them with words.

A standard dictionary gives all the information needed about a word - its spelling, its meaning, where it comes from and how it is used. There are also other smaller dictionaries which list only spellings. These can be very useful for quick reference and they are usually easier to carry round. All dictionaries and most reference books list words in alphabetical order. Alphabet skills are vital for independent learning and *Spelling Worksheets* gives plenty of opportunities for practising them.

This sheet highlights some of the information a standard dictionary gives and it should help with many of the exercises in the worksheets.

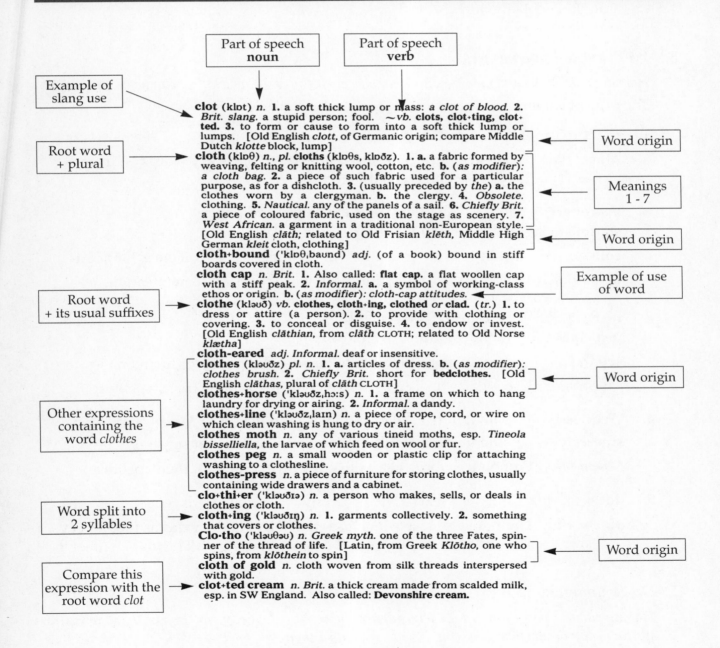

This is an extract from **Collins English Dictionary**

Mnemonics

> **mnemonic** Origin: Greek: *mnemonikos* from *mnemon* (mindful), from *mnasthai* (to remember)
>
> Mnemonics are memory aids or tricks. They can be used to help us to remember spellings of all kinds, especially the awkward ones. Each person has their own collection of special mnemonics for certain spellings but there are many which have become popular because they seem to work well with everyone.

A   *First things first*

1.   A mnemonic for how to **say** *mnemonic* is to link it with *write; know; psychology.* Can you explain why?

2.   A mnemonic for how to **spell** *mnemonic* is to link it with *autumn; column; hymn.* Can you explain why?

B   *Well-known mnemonics*

Here are 5 different mnemonics with examples of spellings for which they can be useful. Try each one out on a spelling which you find hard to remember.

1.   **practice** (noun)   **practise** (verb)   **licence** (noun)   **license** (verb)

   Mnemonic: Remember **advice** *(noun)*   **advise** *(verb)* as key words because they are pronounced differently.

2.   **stationery** *(noun)*   a station**er** sells **e**nvelopes and pap**er**
   stationary *(verb)*   a station**a**ry **c**ar st**a**nds still

   college   a coll**e**ge is for **e**ducation   **collage**   coll**a**ge is for **a**rtists
   Mnemonic: Use letters or letter patterns in words which link in meaning.

3.   **piece** *(a part* or *a portion)*   a p**ie**ce of p**ie**

   principal   Try to think of the Princip**al** as a p**al**!

   separate   If p**a**rents se**pa**rate, **pa** has to pay the going **rate** for maintenance
   Mnemonic: Use whole words within a word to sort out the tricky spelling.

4.   **Wednesday**   split it into 3 syllables and say it differently: Wed - nes - day
   sincerely   split it into 2 words and say it differently: since - rely
   Mnemonic: Pronounce words in a different way to highlight their spelling.

5.   **does**   <u>d</u>og <u>o</u>n <u>e</u>very <u>s</u>eat   **any**   <u>A</u>nne <u>n</u>eeds <u>y</u>ou
   Mnemonic: Think up a phrase which uses the letters of the word as first letters. The odder or more personal it is, the easier it will be to remember.

C   *Do-it-yourself*

The mnemonics you think up for yourself are the best.   Choose one or two of these awkward spellings and decide how you would try to remember them.

   exercise   heart   paid   surprise   said   they   because

Plurals: Words which end in *y*

> **BASIC RULE FOR MAKING A PLURAL**
> The plural of most words is made by adding *-s*.   *NEVER* add *'s* to make a plural.
> If possible, look the word up in a dictionary. It will give the plural of a word if it is unusual.
> **EXCEPTIONS**
> 1.   When a word ends in a consonant + *y* (*e.g. -ty / -ry / -dy*), the plural is spelt by changing the *y* to *i* and adding *-es*. (*e.g. body / bodies; cherry / cherries*).
> 2.   When the word is the name of a person (*Mary; McCarthy*), don't change it - just add *-s*. (*e.g. I saw the two Marys this morning; the McCarthys are coming for tea*)

Fill each gap with the correct plural of the word in brackets.

1.   Book now for our fantastic Italian Bargain Break! Rome, Florence and Venice - 3 _____ (*city*) in 3 _____ (*day*) ! Or if you have more time on your hands, why not try our *Grand Tour of Europe* . Choose any 4 _____ (*country*) in Europe to visit in a 14-day holiday of a lifetime!

2.   Many _____ (*university*) now provide learning _____ (*opportunity*) for people who want to spend their _____ (*holiday*) following up special interests or _____ (*hobby*) .

3.   The Hopton Sports Centre organises a range of _____ (*activity*) for all ages; even _____ (*baby*) can learn to swim. There's Keep Fit for both _____ (*lady*) and men athletics training for girls and _____ (*boy*) . School _____ (*party*) can be accommodated on _____ (*weekday*) with a few hours' notice.

4.   British Rail regrets to announce _____ (*delay*) to train services on the main Edinburgh to Newcastle line due to snow _____ (*flurry*) overnight.

5.   In the week before Christmas, supermarkets always heave with _____ (*body*). The aisles are jammed with _____ (*trolley*) loaded with panic _____ (*buy*). Frozen _____ (*turkey*) are piled next to jars of _____ (*cranberry*). Kids pick up packets of _____ (*Smarty*). Sales _____ (*lady*) in fancy outfits offer shoppers _____ (*tray*) of tasty _____ (*freeby*) to tempt them to buy extra _____ (*goody*) they don't need.

6.   The _____ (*Hardy*) had owned the old house for three _____ (*century*) but the present owner was in his _____ (*eighty*) and had no heir. It was a sad day for the people of the _____ (*valley*) when the smoke from its _____ (*chimney*) died away and the _____ (*key*) of the house were handed over to a developer looking for new sites for _____ (*quarry*) .

WRITING   1.   Make up a shopping list including at least 5 items ending in *-ies* or *-ys*.
             2.   Go round your local supermarket and make a list of brand names which end in *-ies*.

Plurals: -s or -es ?

A   Word puzzle

The answers to the clues are all plurals of words which end in o. Fill them in.

1. Camera pictures
2. A pub game
3. Tapes of TV programmes or films
4. They used to be called *wirelesses*
5. Salad vegetables used in soups and sauces
6. Short for *discotheques*
7. Repeated sounds often heard in caves
8. They can wash hair, cars and carpets

Put the answers in the puzzle into 3 groups according to the way they form their plural.
Add a few other words to each group.

B   How does it sound?

Make each of the words in the gaps plural by adding -s or-es.

Do you ever dream of living some day on an island in the South Pacific? An island where there are golden _____ (beach), with children in _____ (T-shirt) and _____ (short) or cotton _____ (dress), playing on the _____ (sand). An island where you can get away from the _____ (mass) and _____ (thing) like _____ (car), _____ (truck) and _____ (bus); _____ (clock) and _____ (watch); phone calls and _____ (fax); letters and _____ (bill) and _____ (demand) for more _____ (tax). Do you see yourself walking along _____ (path) through _____ (patch) of _____ (rush), eating fresh _____ (peach) and listening to the _____ (buzz) of bees as they pick their way amongst the _____ (bush)? Real life in such _____ (place) is not always so perfect - but it doesn't stop us having our dreams.

List the words from the gaps in two groups: -s endings and -es endings. Say the -es list aloud. Can you hear why these words all have -es in their plural?

Plurals: Oddities

BASIC RULE FOR MAKING A PLURAL

The plural of most words is made by adding *-s*.   *NEVER* add *'s* to make a plural.
If possible, look the word up in a dictionary. It will give the plural of a word if it is unusual.

EXCEPTIONS

Some words are odd when it comes to their plural. They change their last letter or their middle letters and sometimes they don't change at all.

A   Words ending in -f or -fe

Some of these titles might be found on the shelves of your local library. All the missing words are the plural of a word which ends in -f or -fe. Can you fill in the blanks?

1.   The Six _____ of Henry VIII   *History*

2.   _____ : *The Story of a Football Club*   *Sport*

3.   Winter Knitting 1. *Hats,* _____ *and Gloves*   *Crafts*

4.   Robin Hood-Prince of _____   *Films*

5.   Night of the Long _____   *Modern History*

6.   Five _____ and two small fishes: *The miracles of Jesus*   *Religion*

7.   Rearing Cows and _____   *Farming*

8.   The Time of our _____   *Biography*

9.   Know your trees by their _____   *Natural History*

10. Two _____ make a whole   *Mathematics*

   Remember: *The plural of **roof** is **roofs**:   the plural of **handkerchief** is **handkerchiefs***

B   What's the plural?

Write down the plural of each of these words, then say which is the odd one out in each group.

1.   man   woman   human   gentleman
2.   foot   goose   boot   tooth
3.   salmon   cod   sprat   mackerel
4.   spinach   broccoli   leek   parsley

<table>
<tr><td>

Which is the odd one out in each line?

| trousers | shoes | tights | pyjamas |
| scissors | pliers | nails | shears |

</td><td>

Write down the plural of each word

| house | mouse | spouse |
| | louse | grouse |

</td></tr>
</table>

WRITING   *Make a list of 10 items in the room you are sitting in and write down the plural of each. Write a short description of the room including as many of the items on your list as you can.*

Plurals: Collective nouns

Collective nouns are single words which describe more than one of anything.
e.g. the Government is a group or collection of *M.P. s, Peers etc.*
a swarm is a collection of *bees*

A One for all

Write down the collective noun for each of these. There is often more than one answer.

1. a large number of people
2. eleven cricketers or footballers
3. a group of musicians
4. a group of soldiers
5. a collection of books
6. an association of workers
7. a group of stars
8. a group of trees
9. a number of cattle
10. a number of playing cards

B How many?

What number does each of these words represent?

1. a couple
2. a century
3. a quartet
4. triplets
5. a decade
6. a pair

7. a bicycle
8. a triangle
9. an octagon
10. a pentathlon
11. a dozen
12. an item

Add some more of your own.

C Initials

What groups of people do these initials represent?

1. BBC
2. WI
3. GEC
4. NHS
5. AA
6. TUC
7. RAF
8. UN

WRITING *Write a newspaper report which includes some of these collective nouns:*

committee   police   council   board   army

Prefixes (1)

Many longer words are made up of at least three distinct parts - a prefix, a root and a suffix. Adding a prefix or a suffix is often a quick way of changing the meaning of a root word.

e.g. **un** (*prefix*) + **employ** (*root*) + **ment** (*suffix*) = **unemployment**

A **prefix** is a group of letters with a meaning of its own which comes at the beginning of a word. Most prefixes came originally from either Latin or Greek.

❏ Knowing the meanings of some of the most common prefixes can help you to guess at the meanings of new words.

❏ Knowing the spellings of common prefixes can help you to break down longer words into parts which are easier to learn.

A Before and after

pre- means *before*   **post-** means *after*

Fill each gap with one of the above prefixes and give the meaning of each word.

_____ fix	_____ pone	_____ position
_____ pare	_____ fer	_____ mortem
_____ natal	_____ school	_____ packed
_____ paid	_____ dated	_____ graduate
_____ humous	_____ cooked	_____ shrunk

B What do they mean?

Look up these prefixes in a standard dictionary to find their meanings and the language they come from.

inter-   **trans-**   **over-**

Write down 5 words which begin with each of the prefixes.

C One or many?

a. The prefix **uni-** means **one**
What do these words mean?

1. uniform
2. unit
3. unilateral
4. unique
5. unisex

b. The prefix **multi-** means **many**
What do these words mean?

1. multiply
2. multi-storey
3. multi-media
4. multitude
5. multi-purpose

Add more words to each group.

WRITING

Write a piece with the title: **That's Life!**
Include as many words as possible which contain prefixes from this sheet.

Prefixes (2)

Many longer words are made up of at least three distinct parts - a prefix, a root and a suffix. Adding a prefix or a suffix is often a quick way of changing the meaning of a root word.

e.g.   **un** *(prefix)* + **employ** *(root)* + **ment** *(suffix)* = **unemployment**

A **prefix** is a group of letters with a meaning of its own which comes at the beginning of a word. Most prefixes came originally from either Latin or Greek.

❑   Knowing the meanings of some of the most common prefixes can help you to guess at the meanings of new words.

❑   Knowing the spellings of common prefixes can help you to break down longer words into parts which are easier to learn.

A   Opposites

un-   dis-   de-

Add one of the prefixes above to each of the words below to make it mean the opposite:

do	appear	value	agree
freeze	like	fair	code
dress	bug	approve	known
expected	advantage	skilled	true

Think of some more words with these prefixes. Do they always make words into opposites?

B   Word puzzle

Many words begin with the prefix **re-**. *Fill in the puzzle.*

1. Play it again!
2. Say it again
3. Go back (or come back)
4. Do up something old
5. Think of the past
6. Drive backwards
7. Jog the memory
8. Swot for an exam

Make up your own puzzle like this one, using other words beginning with **re-**.

C   Prefixes as words

Many prefixes are used in everyday expressions, often as words in their own right.
What do these mean? Write them in full if they are abbreviations.

p.s.	**P.M.T.**	**sub.**	**ad infinitum**
pros and cons	**re**	**'ex'**	**ad nauseam**
a.m.	**p.m.**	**pp.** *(in a letter)*	**ad lib.**

Prefixes (3)

Many longer words are made up of at least three distinct parts - a prefix, a root and a suffix. Adding a prefix or a suffix is often a quick way of changing the meaning of a root word.

e.g.   **un** *(prefix)* + **employ** *(root)* + **ment** *(suffix)* = **unemployment**

A **prefix** is a group of letters with a meaning of its own which comes at the beginning of a word. Most prefixes came originally from either Latin or Greek.

❏ Knowing the meanings of some of the most common prefixes can help you to guess at the meanings of new words.

❏ Knowing the spellings of common prefixes can help you to break down longer words into parts which are easier to learn.

A   *ad*

*The prefix **ad** means **to** or **towards***

*ad often changes its ending and doubles the first letter of the root it is attached to - usually to make words easier to say.   Look up **ad-** in a standard dictionary to see how it works, then do the exercise below.*

*All the words missing from these sentences begin with the prefix **ad** with its last letter changed according to the root which follows it. Fill in the words.*

1.   She _____ the gift with pleasure.

2.   "We regret to _____ that the _____ of the flight from Brussels will be delayed."

3.   Your next _____ with the dentist is on Friday.

4.   The students' _____ had to be ready for _____ by the end of May.

5.   _____ all passengers! Please do not _____ to leave the train while it is in motion.

6.   Smoking is not _____ in this office.

B   *com, con* and *co*

*The prefixes **com, con** and **co** all have the same meaning - **with; together; jointly***

con and com often drop their last letter and double the first letter of the root which follows them; co stays the same

Fill in the words in this puzzle.

1.   Box to store things in

2.   Person you work with

3.   Care in the _____

4.   An admiring remark

5.   Work together

6.   Talking is a _____ skill

7.   Place for further education

8.   Right; without errors

Prefixes (4)

> Many longer words are made up of at least three distinct parts - a prefix, a root and a suffix. Adding a prefix or a suffix is often a quick way of changing the meaning of a root word.
>
> e.g.   **un** *(prefix)* + **employ** *(root)* + **ment** *(suffix)* = **unemployment**
>
> A **prefix** is a group of letters with a meaning of its own which comes at the beginning of a word. Most prefixes came originally from either Latin or Greek.
>
> ❏ Knowing the meanings of some of the most common prefixes can help you to guess at the meanings of new words.
>
> ❏ Knowing the spellings of common prefixes can help you to break down longer words into parts which are easier to learn.

A   Above and below

sub means **below** or **under** or **lesser**   **super** means **above** or **greater** or **higher**

Give the meanings of these words:

1. submarine
2. subtitle
3. substitute
4. supervisor
5. supersonic
6. superb

7. subscription
8. subtract
9. substandard
10. supermarket
11. supernatural
12. superstition

B   In the beginning

*Put either **sub** or **super** in front of these words:*

man	contractor	total	power
station	star	structure	urban
tanker	human	tax	way

C   Which is which?

sub and super often change or shorten at the beginning of some words.

*Say which prefix (**sub** or **super**) you think has been changed at the beginning of these words. Looking the words up in a standard dictionary will help you to decide.*

1. surplus
2. surname
3. surprise
4. surcharge

5. suffix
6. sufficient
7. suffer
8. support

9. suspect
10. suspend
11. sustain
12. suppress

WRITING   *Write a letter of complaint to a shop or supermarket about a faulty item you have purchased. Use as many **sub** and **super** words from this page as you can.*

Proof reading

Proof reading is the most important skill needed for good spelling and writing. Everyone makes mistakes when writing - with spelling; with grammar; leaving words out, or leaving them in when they shouldn't be there; forgetting to say something essential in a job application. Proof reading is a professional writer's word for re-reading and checking what they have written. A *proof* is a rough printed draft.

No one should write anything without proof reading it. It doesn't matter whether it is a few words on a form, a note to your child's teacher or a letter to a friend. Anyone who reads your writing will understand it better if it is correctly spelt and free of mistakes. And you will get more satisfaction from it, too.

- ☐ Get into the habit of proof reading. Get used to the look of words. Use your eyes!
- ☐ Never write anything without re-reading and checking it, however trivial it may be. If it is an important piece of writing (**e.g.** a business letter or job application) or something which will look bad if it is corrected (**e.g.** a greetings card or a form), write a rough draft on scrap paper and proof read and correct it before writing the proper copy. .
- ☐ Learn to use a dictionary and always have it at hand to help.
- ☐ If you use a computer, don't rely on the Spell Check. It only tells you that a word exists. It won't tell you whether it's the right one for the context in which you have used it.

A   What's wrong?

There is an error in each of these signs. Can you spot it?

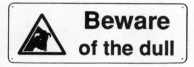

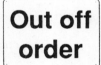

B   Correct the errors

This is a letter in reply to the advertisement on the right.
It contains 12 errors. Can you find them?

Dear Sir or Madam,

I am righting to you about the advertisement in the *Eveing News* on June 8th for a Van Diver/Stores Asistant.

I am aged 20 and I have driving for 2 years. I have a clean license. My work experience since leaving Park End School is:

    Age 16-18: YTS Painting and Decerating (Abbey Training)

    Age 19-20: Part-time Ice-cream Salesman/Driver (Toni's Ices)

I was was made redundant 3 weeks ago, so I coud start imediately I am not on the telephone but you can leave a message with my sister, Mrs. V. Fisher, on 770011.

Your faithfully,

Pat Morris

Roots

Many longer words are made up of at least three distinct parts - a prefix, a root and a suffix. Adding a prefix or a suffix is often a quick way of changing the meaning of a root word.

e.g. **un** *(prefix)* + **employ** *(root)* + **ment** *(suffix)* = **unemployment**

❑ Sometimes the root is a common spelling pattern (usually with a meaning in its original language). Knowing the meanings of some of the most common roots can help you to guess at the meanings of new words.

❑ Sometimes the root is a whole word. Knowing its spelling and meaning can help you to work out the meaning of a longer word which contains it.

A Whole words as roots

How many new words can you make by adding prefixes and suffixes to the words below? Some examples you could use are given in the box.

port (*e.g. re-port-er*)

form

dress

miss

act

fix

Prefixes:	in	un	de	con
	dis	ad	pre	per
	re	ex	im	
Suffixes:	ly	ion	er	ation
	ive	ant	ing	ed

B Common spelling patterns as roots

How many words can you make which include each of the patterns underlined? Add both prefixes and suffixes.

e.g. **-vol-** *can be found in:* **revolve, involve, revolution, evolve, devolve, Volvo**

re<u>ver</u>se   in<u>ven</u>t   <u>voc</u>ation   ex<u>ten</u>d

C Find the root

a. *Use a standard dictionary to find the root that each of these groups of words has in common.*

b. *What does the root word mean and which language does it come from?*

c. *How does the meaning of the root word fit into the meaning of each word in the group?*

1. script   scripture   describe   prescription

2. receive   reception   except   recipé   deceit

3. dictionary   addict   dictator   prediction

4. education   introduce   conductor   viaduct

5. direct   directory   correction   rector

Add another word with the same root to each group.

eigh or aigh ?

eigh and *aigh* usually sound the same, but one or two common words containing *eigh* are pronounced differently and just have to be learned.

A   Choose the right word

Choose a word from the box for each of the clues below.

weight	eight	Neighbours	freight	neigh	sleigh

1. Popular TV soap opera about good friends.
2. Goods carried by road, rail or air.
3. Transport for snowy weather - especially at Christmas?
4. It can be measured in pounds or kilograms.
5. The number in 4 pairs.
6. A horse's laugh?

B   What's the difference?

1. Way in
2. Weigh in

C   Which is the odd one out?

1. weigh   sleigh   neigh   way
2. eight   height   weight   freight
3. neighbour   weighed   sleigh   straight
4. Leigh-on-Sea   Budleigh Salterton   Keighley   Stoneleigh

D   What do they mean?

Explain each of these words and phrases by putting them into a sentence:

1. the straight and narrow
2. go straight
3. a straight fight
4. straight, no chaser
5. straight up
6. the home straight
7. a straight flush
8. a straightedge
9. a straight face
10. straightaway

WRITING

Write a sports report for a newspaper with one of these headlines:

Green Timber stumbles in the home straight *(Horse racing)*

Thunderball Jackson 5 lbs overweight *(Boxing)*

Tenku makes it into the last eight *(Athletics)*

igh (1)

igh sounds like *I* or *eye*. The *gh* is always silent.
Words with this spelling pattern are often confused with words which sound the same but have a different spelling and meaning *(e.g. sight and site)*. Words like this are called *homophones* and there are a lot of them in English. It is important to learn both their meaning and their spelling at the same time.

A   Word puzzle

All the answers to the clues below have igh in them. Fit them into the squares.

1. Not wrong
2. Not low
3. Not heavy
4. Not day
5. Not dim
6. Not loose
7. Not big
8. Not the whole leg

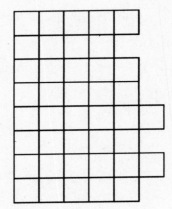

B   What's the difference?

Put each of these homophones in a sentence which explains its meaning:

1. sight   site
2. might   mite

3. right   rite
4. wright   write

C   Songs of Praise

Here are some extracts from well-known carols and hymns. Fill in the gaps with words containing igh.

1. Silent _____ , Holy _____ ,
   All is calm, all is _____ .

2. Good King Wenceslas looked out
   On the feast of Stephen.
   When the snow lay round about,
   Deep and crisp and even.
   _____ shone the moon that _____ .
   Though the frost was cruel,
   When a poor man came in _____ .
   Gath'ring winter fuel.

3. _____ the good _____ with all thy _____ .
   Christ is thy strength and Christ thy _____ .

Can you think of any other songs with igh words in them?

igh (2)

> ***igh*** sounds like ***I*** or ***eye***. The ***gh*** is always silent.
> Words with this spelling pattern are often confused with words which sound the same but have a different spelling and meaning (***e.g. sight*** and ***site***). Words like this are called *homophones* and there are a lot of them in English. It is important to learn both their meaning and their spelling at the same time.

A Is it right?

*Advertisers often mis-spell well-known words to attract attention to the products they are selling. Words with **igh** in them are easy targets. What is the correct spelling for each of these?*

Ultrabrite   Startrite   Nite Lite   Flo-Lite   Hi Lites

B Fill in the blanks

*All the missing words in this extract from a holiday brochure have **igh** in them. Fill them in.*

Christmas is over and the weather's cold. Now's the time to _____ up those long, dark winter _____ with our Summer Sun holiday brochure. See the _____ in Rome and Athens. Scale the snowy _____ of the Swiss Alps or dive into the depths of a tropical lagoon. It's never too soon to start planning the _____ of a break in the sun. We run daily _____ to all parts of the world and we'll fix up a package that is just _____ for you. Don't be _____ to ask our friendly travel assistants for advice. They _____ just surprise you with their attention to even the _____ detail. You'll give a _____ of relief that you chose Suntours to give you your _____ holiday ever.

Which of the missing spellings is the odd one out?

C What do you mean?

Explain the difference in meaning between these pairs of words:

1. a night and a knight
2. a light and alight
3. lightning and lightening
4. tight and tights
5. slight and sleight

> **Q.** Why do dragons sleep in the daytime?
> **A.** So that they can fight knights.

WRITING   *Write a piece with one of these titles. Use as many **igh** words as you can.*

It'll be all right on the night   Moonlight and Roses

Women's rights   The Highway Code

ough *(as in rough)*

The letters *ough* can be used to represent 7 different sounds in English. It is probably easiest to learn words containing each sound in groups and try to find an everyday context or mnemonic to help in remembering them.

Usually there are only a few words containing each sound, but they are often common ones.

A Fill in the blanks

1. It's _____ at the top.

2. You have to take the _____ with the smooth.

3. "Have you had _____ ?"

4. The meat was as _____ as old boots.

5. _____ is as good as a feast.

B Well-known phrases

Make up sentences containing each of these phrases:

oddly enough   soon enough   that's enough   good enough

fair enough   enough said   far enough   right enough   sure enough

Add more of your own.

C Cutting up rough

What do these words and phrases mean? Put each one into a sentence.

1. rough and ready
2. the rough *(golf)*
3. roughage
4. a rough diamond
5. to ride rough-shod over
6. a rough ride

7. to rough it
8. to rough up
9. rough-cast
10. rough justice
11. a rough draft
12. to sleep rough

WRITING

Using words from the box for the rhymes, make up a limerick beginning with one of the lines below:

a. There was a young lady from Brough........

b. There was a footballer named Clough........

A limerick is a 5-line poem, in which lines 1, 2 & 5 rhyme with each other and lines 3 & 4 rhyme with each other. It follows a set rhythm and it is usually funny.

Note: *There is an example of a limerick on p. 27*

rough	scuff	enough
gruff	chough	stuff
tough	puff	cuff
huff	bluff	snuff
duff	fluff	muff
scruff	buff	chuffed

ough *(as in through)*

The letters *ough* can be used to represent 7 different sounds in English. It is probably easiest to learn words containing each sound in groups and try to find an everyday context or mnemonic to help in remembering them.

Usually there are only a few words containing each sound, but they are often common ones.

A   Complete these sentences *(through / throughout)*

1.   ....throughout the night.
2.   ....through no fault of my own.
3.   ....but he got through in the end.
4.   People throughout the world........
5.   ....throughout the holiday period.
6.   ....through the bathroom window.
7.   The path went through........
8.   ....central heating throughout.

B   Homophones

*The words **through** and **threw** are often confused because they sound the same. The easiest way of remembering the difference between them is that **threw** is a verb, and only a verb. **Through** can be used in many ways, but not as a verb.*

1.   ***Explain these expressions***

No through road   through-put   follow through

a breakthrough   a through train   Monday through Friday

2.   ***Put these phrasal verbs into sentences***

threw out   threw over   threw at   threw away

threw into   threw in   threw together   threw off

C   Fill in the blanks *(through / throughout / threw)*

The tennis champion had been a hard hitter _____ his career, both on and off the court. Most tennis fans thought he was rotten _____ and _____ . This was his last match. He smashed the ball hard over the net. It went straight _____ and hit the line judge in the chest. She _____ the ball back, though she looked pretty sick. For the next few points, she seemed just to be going _____ the motions. "If this is what it's like being a line judge," she thought, "I'm _____ with it!"

At the end of the match, the champion _____ down his racquet and ran over to apologise to her. Although she was pleased that he had taken the trouble, she still _____ up when she got into the changing room.

ough (as in though)

The letters *ough* can be used to represent 7 different sounds in English. It is probably easiest to learn words containing each sound in groups and try to find an everyday context or mnemonic to help in remembering them.

Usually there are only a few words containing each sound, but they are often common ones.

A   Complete these sentences   (though / although)

1. She was already a good tap dancer _____ she was only five years old.

2. Even _____ he was rushed to hospital after the accident, he was dead on arrival.

3. "My husband's a good cook. He's not keen on shopping, _____ ."

4. They went to see the film again, even _____ they had seen it twice before.

5. She was very upset, _____ she tried not to show it.

6. His jeans are so tight, he looks as _____ he's been poured into them.

7. _____ he had trained hard for the marathon, he only managed 20 miles.

8. She felt so ill that she went home, _____ it was only 2 o'clock.

9. "My mother's a good driver. She's useless at car maintenance, _____ ."

10. "I still can't remember that spelling, _____ I've tried every way I can think of."

11. _____ there were only four people there, the Council meeting started on time.

12. "Tomorrow will be dry and sunny, _____ there may be rain overnight."

13. He was over seventy, _____ he looked 20 years younger.

14. Her face was so white, she looked as _____ she'd seen a ghost.

15. The horse came last in the race, even _____ he'd been tipped to win.

B   What does it mean?

Write sentences showing the different meanings of the word **dough**.

Did you know?

Everyone knows what a **doughnut** *is. But did you know that, in 1989, when television cameras were first allowed into the House of Commons, M.P. s invented a new activity. It is now called* **doughnutting**. *Whenever a member is televised addressing the House, other M.P. s sit in a close ring (the shape of a doughnut) round him or her. This gives viewers the impression that the House is full when, in fact, it may be almost empty.*

WRITING

Write notes for what you would say if you had to give a demonstration of making one of these. Try it out on your family or a group at your college or centre.

1. a loaf and some bread rolls
2. some ring and some jammy doughnuts
3. a pizza
4. a batch of scones

ough *(as in cough)* & ough *(as in Slough)*

> The letters *ough* can be used to represent 7 different sounds in English. It is probably easiest to learn words containing each sound in groups and try to find an everyday context or mnemonic to help in remembering them.
>
> Usually there are only a few words containing each sound, but they are often common ones.

A   ough *(as in cough)*

cough and *trough* are two words in which *ough* sounds like *off*. There are very few other words like them and they are mostly the names of people or places.

1. What is a drinking trough?

2. What is a trough of low pressure?

3. What and where is the Trough of Bowland?

4. Frank Bough is a TV personality; Roger McGough is a poet. What do their names have in common?

5. Can you think of any other people's names or place-names which have *ough* (as in *cough*) in them?

6. What is a hiccough, and how do you say it?

B   ough *(as in Slough)*

1. *Poems which rhyme can be a good way of remembering odd spellings and their sounds. This is the first verse of a poem written by John Betjeman in 1937:*

    Slough
    Come, friendly bombs, and fall on Slough
    It isn't fit for humans now,
    There isn't grass to graze a cow
    Swarm over, Death!

    Write down the words in the verse which end with the same sound as **Slough**.

2. *These two words are homophones. Put each word in a sentence to show the difference in their meaning:*

    bough   **bow**

WRITING   *Here is an example of a limerick:*

There was an old man from the Tyne,
Who got drunk on a bottle of wine.
He sat down in the square.
The police found him there
And they gave him a very large fine.

Using some of the words from the box as rhymes, make up a limerick beginning:

There was an old person from Slough.......

bough	now	how
plough	row	vow
allow	cow	brow

ough *(as in borough)*

The letters *ough* can be used to represent 7 different sounds in English. It is probably easiest to learn words containing each sound in groups and try to find an everyday context or mnemonic to help in remembering them.

Usually there are only a few words containing each sound, but they are often common ones.

This pattern and sound is found most often in place-names because it is in the word *borough*, meaning fort or fortified place.

A **Fill in the endings of these names of towns and cities in England and Scotland with -borough, -brough, or -burgh:**

Scar_____

Middles_____

Helens_____

Farn_____ *(Hants.)*

Welling_____

Edin_____

Lough_____

Peter_____

Jed_____

Put the above places on the map.

B **Using an atlas**

1. *Using a road atlas, find one or two more place-names with any of the endings in A above.*

2. *Other word endings with the same meaning as* **borough** *are* **-bury, -berry** *and* **-bergh**. *How many places with any of these endings can you find in the atlas?*

C **Word origins**

The words **thorough** *and* **through** *both come from the same Old English word:* **thurh**.

1. *In the UK, we have* **thoroughfares**; *in the USA, they have* **throughways**. *What are they?*

2. *Give another meaning for the word* **thorough**.

WRITING **a.** *Choose one of the places mentioned above and plan out a weekend break there. Say why you chose the place and what you would do there.*

b. *Write a post card to a friend from the place you have chosen for your weekend break.*

Brown and Brown / Spelling Worksheets

ough or augh ?

The letters *ough* can be used to represent 7 different sounds in English. It is probably easiest to learn words containing each sound in groups and try to find an everyday context or mnemonic to help in remembering them.

Usually there are only a few words containing each sound, but they are often common ones.

A   What's the word?

*All the answers to these clues are words which contain **ought** or **aught**.*
Write the words in the box.

1. Zero
2. Badly behaved
3. Something you think
4. Sounds like *fort*
5. Female child
6. Abattoir
7. Opposite of *sold*
8. Sounds like *court*

			G	H							
			G	H							
				G	H						
			G	H							
			G	H							
				G	H						
			G	H							
			G	H							

B   Odd one out

*In some words, **ough** and **augh** are pronounced differently. Say each group of words aloud and decide which word is the odd one out.*

1. cough   laugh   trough

2. taught   daughter   laughter   manslaughter

3. brought   ought   sought   draught

List the 3 odd words out. Underline the sound and spelling they have in common.

C   Homophones

What is the difference in meaning between these pairs of words?

1. draught   draft
2. sought   sort
3. caught   court
4. fought   fort
5. taught   taut

WRITING   *Write a short piece with one of these titles:*

   The Last Laugh   Sons or Daughters?   Thought for the day

The *sh* sound

> The sound which is most often spelt *sh* can also be spelt: **ci   ti   si   ssi   ch**
> Many everyday words contain one of these spelling patterns, so they are worth sorting out.

A   Pick out the spelling pattern

*Underline all the words in this piece which contain a **sh** sound.*

Politicians claim that there is a special relationship between Britain and the United States which is essential to the U.K.'s position in the world. Officials in both countries often have confidential talks before taking action on certain issues. There is some tension about this among members of the European Commission who think that the U.S.'s obsession with power is a potential danger to international co-operation.

Group the words you have underlined according to the spelling pattern they contain.
Add another word to each group which contains the same spelling and sound.

B   Hear the difference

*All these words contain **ch**. Underline the words which contain **ch** as in **machine**.*

chef	cheese	chocolate	creche	chips	march
church	champagne	moustache	teacher		Michelle
much	chicken	Chanel No. 5	channel		chauffeur
cheque	chic	arch	brochure	quiche	Charles

Which language do many of the words you have underlined come from?

WRITING

1. *Write a piece giving your views on the N.H.S., using some of the words from the box.*

prescription	depression	physician	National
optician	artificial	prevention	patient
operation	partial	efficient	permission

2. *Write a love story with one of these titles:*

   A Passionate Affair   Possession   Charlotte in Russia

   The Fruits of Passion   Delicious Passion

30

Brown and Brown / Spelling Worksheets

The *ur* sound (1)

The **ur** sound is one of the most common sounds in English, mainly because it can be spelt in so many ways:

ur   er   ar   ir   or   our   ear   re   ure   eur

❐ To spell an *ur* sound correctly in a word, you must remember what the word looks like and what it means. Try to picture it in your mind's eye and link it with other words which have the same spelling and sound.

A   How many?

Read this piece.   How many **ur** *sounds does it contain?*

To spell an *ur* sound in a word correctly, you must remember what the word looks like and what it means. Where have you seen the word before? Do you see it often in the shops, on a street sign, in the place where you work or at the centre or college you attend? It doesn't matter how you say it. The word **looks** the same whether you live in Blackburn or Aberdeen or Birmingham or Bangor and that's what matters when you have to write it down.

Once you have learned the spelling of the *ur* sound in a word you use or see often and you can picture it in your mind's eye, you can link it up with other words that contain the same spelling of that sound and try to keep them in your mind as a group.

Make a list of all the words in the piece which contain an **ur** *sound.*

B   Which looks right?

Here are 12 common words. Fill in each blank with one of these:

ur   ir   ear   or   our   ar   er

1. Sat____day
2. b____thday
3. ex____cise
4. Woolw____th

5. neighb____
6. ____ly
7. w____d
8. Lab____

9. station____
10. w____e
11. gramm____
12. f____st

Say when and where you last saw each word.

C   Which is the odd one out?

1. learn   earn   urn   earnest
2. Spurs   Rangers   Everton   Rovers
3. robber   murderer   burglar   prisoner
4. teacher   trainer   supervisor   organiser

WRITING   *Write a short piece with one of these titles:*

1. For better, for worse.
2. Say it with flowers.
3. The early bird catches the worm.

The *ur* sound (2)

The **ur** sound is one of the most common sounds in English, mainly because it can be spelt in so many ways:

ur	er	ar	ir	or	our	ear	re	ure	eur

❐ To spell an *ur* sound correctly in a word, you must remember what the word looks like and what it means. Try to picture it in your mind's eye and link it with other words which have the same spelling and sound.

A Place-names

Add 2 or more place-names which contain the same spelling of the **ur** *sound as each of these:*

1. Blackburn   2. Aberdeen   3. Birmingham   4. Bangor

B What's the difference?

These pairs of words are homophones. They sound the same but they have different spellings and meanings. Use each word in a sentence to show the difference between them.

1. earn   urn
2. heard   herd
3. pearl   purl
4. earnest   Ernest

5. birth   berth
6. fir   fur
7. turn   tern

C In the picture

Fill in the answers to the clues. All the words end in **ure**.

1. Chairs, tables and beds, for example
2. Spare time
3. The main film is often called this
4. Enjoyment
5. A talk or speech
6. A grassy field for animals to feed in
7. Opposite of *income*
8. Very small

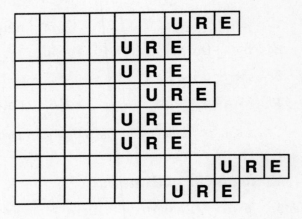

WRITING   *Choose one of the sets of words below and write a story which includes them.*

A

Inspector	murder	first
search	procedure	revolver

B

actor	curtain	performance
picture	director	theatre

The *ur* sound (3)

The **ur** sound is one of the most common sounds in English, mainly because it can be spelt in so many ways:

|ur|er|ar|ir|or|our|ear|re|ure|eur|

❑ To spell an *ur* sound correctly in a word, you must remember what the word looks like and what it means. Try to picture it in your mind's eye and link it with other words which have the same spelling and sound.

A How many?

*Read this piece, then write down all the words with an **ur** sound in them.*

A first-rate young hurdler urgently needed a sponsor to help her to go further in her sport. Her trainer at the Sports Centre had heard that a local firm was searching for someone to support. He had a word with the Managing Director who preferred her because he would only venture money on a young person who was a certain winner. He wanted his firm's name featured on the girl's kit so that it would be seen every time she appeared at athletics fixtures all over the world.

"I've got no burning interest in sport," the Director said. "All I want is a nice little earner. Otherwise, it's not worth the bother."

List the words in groups according to the spelling pattern they contain.
Which patterns come at the end of a word? Are there any which don't?

B What's the difference?

These pairs of words are homonyms. They are spelt the same way, but they have different meanings.

Use each word in a sentence to show the different meanings.

1. burn   burn
2. stern   stern
3. purse   purse
4. turn   turn
5. churn   churn

WRITING   *Choose one of the sets of words below and write a news report which includes them.*

A		
nurse	doctor	Infirmary
stretcher	recovery	injury

B		
church	hearse	earth
verger	vicar	funeral

The *ur* sound (4)

The **ur** sound is one of the most common sounds in English, mainly because it can be spelt in so many ways:

> ur   er   ar   ir   or   our   ear   re   ure   eur

❏ To spell an *ur* sound correctly in a word, you must remember what the word looks like and what it means. Try to picture it in your mind's eye and link it with other words which have the same spelling and sound.

Blame the French

*Many words which contain **our** came into English from France. The French thought they were improving our language by bringing in more 'refined' words.*

Use the clues below to help you to find the **our** *words in the Word Search Square.*

(The words are fitted in horizontally, vertically and diagonally, but not upside down!)

```
H O L A B O U R J N M G
E P A R L O U R O E S F
W H U M O U R T U I D A
T A O O V S T I R G A V
A R D U A I P L N H J O
S B O R L N G C A B O U
A O U P O T C O L O U R
V U R B U G N D U U R S
I R S M R U M O U R N L
O V O I L E T J S S E D
U U F L A V O U R L Y K
R A T B E H A V I O U R
```

1. Fun.
2. A smell.
3. A trip from one place to another.
4. Newspaper or magazine.
5. Work.
6. *e.g.* Red, green or blue.
7. A sheltered port.
8. Bravery.
9. Gossip or hearsay.
10. Old-fashioned protective suit for battle.
11. Old-fashioned word for a sitting-room.
12. Health and strength.
13. People who live next door.
14. Manners.
15. A person who rescues someone from danger.
16. A good turn.
17. An abnormal swelling, often in the brain.
18. The taste of food.

WRITING   *Write out one of your favourite recipés to enter for a magazine competition called* **Reader's Flavour of the Month**. *Include some of the words from the box below:*

sugar	savoury	burger	mixture	butter
stir	temperature	casserole	freezer	supper

would / could / should (1)

> would, could and should are parts of a verb. No other words in English contain -ould with the same sound and spelling. Learn them together and always think of them as a threesome. Note that the *l* is silent.
>
> ❏ **would not   could not   should not**
>   are often shortened to **wouldn't   couldn't   shouldn't**
>
> ❏ **I would   he would   she would   it would   we would   you would   they would**
>   are often shortened to **I'd   he'd   she'd   it'd   we'd   you'd   they'd**

A   Fill in the blanks (would / could / should)

1.   I _____ be grateful if you _____ send me your catalogue.

2.   Please _____ you collect your parcel from the Parcels Office?

3.   "If I had a bike, I _____ get there quicker."

4.   "I know I _____ go to the meeting, but I don't feel like it."

5.   "I _____ if I _____ , but I can't!"

6.   "If you _____ move over, I _____ sit down!"

B   Fill in the blanks (wouldn't / couldn't / shouldn't)

1.   She _____ go swimming because her leg was in plaster.

2.   "You _____ do that if the boss was here!"

3.   "Sorry to have kept you waiting, but it _____ be long now."

4.   "_____ you do that later? Your dinner's getting cold."

5.   "She _____ come, even if I begged her."

6.   "You _____ be doing that - not in your spare time."

C   Song titles

This is the first line of a song. Fill in the blank and give the title.

"What _____ you do if I sang out of tune......?"

Think of some more song titles or first lines which contain
would/wouldn't, could/couldn't, *or* **should/shouldn't.**

D   Finish the sentence

Make up some sentences beginning with this phrase:

He couldn't organise.........

Here lies John Bunn
Who was killed by a gun.
His name wasn't Bunn,
But Wood.
But Wood
Wouldn't rhyme with gun
And Bunn would.

WRITING   *a. Write your reply to a formal wedding or party invitation.*

b. Write a piece starting: If I could have my time over again.......

would / could / should (2)

> *would, could* and *should* are parts of a verb. No other words in English contain *-ould* with the same sound and spelling. Learn them together and always think of them as a threesome. Note that the *l* is silent.
>
> ☐ *would not   could not   should not*
>   are often shortened to *wouldn't   couldn't   shouldn't*
>
> ☐ *I would   he would   she would   it would   we would   you would   they would*
>   are often shortened to *I'd   he'd   she'd   it'd   we'd   you'd   they'd*

A   Write out the words in italics in full

1. "*I'd* like to have a night out this week".
2. "If *he'd* only think first, *he'd* make fewer mistakes."
3. "*I'd* be pleased if *you'd* come to the hospital with me."
4. "She *wouldn't* take 'No' for an answer."
5. "I *shouldn't* have been so rude, but I *couldn't* help it."
6. "*It'd* be great if *you'd* see it my way, just for once!"

B   Fill in the blanks

Would you? Could you? Should you?

What _____ you do if there was a fire in your home? _____ you cope with it on your own? Where _____ you go for help? Did you know that you _____ try to put out an electrical fire with water? What if someone was injured? _____ you try to move someone if you thought they had a broken leg? Many people think that they _____ know what to do, but they forget that they _____ be in a panic and probably _____ react as they normally _____ .

If you _____ like to be cool, calm and collected in an emergency, you _____ think about joining a First Aid class. For more details, you _____ ring your local Adult Education Centre.

C   Answer and question

*Here are the answers to some questions. Write out the questions, including **would, could** or **should** in each question.*

1. "I'd like a pint of bitter, please."
2. "It would be nice to go to the beach."
3. "On Thursday."
4. "Only if I've got nothing better to do."
5. "Why not? You'd be good at it."

Suffixes (1)

Many longer words are made up of at least three distinct parts - a prefix, a root and a suffix. Adding a prefix or a suffix is often a quick way of changing the meaning of a root word.

e.g.   **un** *(prefix)* + **employ** *(root)* + **ment** *(suffix)* = **unemployment**

A **suffix** is a group of letters added to the end of a word. Sometimes the end of the root word is changed before the suffix is added. This often makes the word easier to say and it can also show the difference between two words with similar spellings.

A   *Words ending in a consonant + y*

*When a word ends with a **consonant** + y, change the **y** to **i** before adding a suffix.*

❐ **Exception:** *If the suffix begins with **i**, keep the **y**, to avoid having double **i**.*

How many of the suffixes in the box can you add to each of the words below?

es	ed	ing	est	er	ly
fy	ful	ness	day	ment	less

busy	lazy	cry
holy	try	beauty
happy	early	fry
fly	tidy	supply
pretty	dry	reply

B   *Words ending in silent e*

*If the suffix to be added begins with a vowel, take off the **e** before adding the ending.*
*If the suffix to be added begins with a consonant, keep the **e**.*

How many of the suffixes in the box above can you add to each of these words?

write	improve	care
sincere	use	dine
love	late	like
hope	arrange	safe

WRITING

1. Write a list of all the different ways you can 'sign off' a letter by starting with **Yours** ....

2. Write a formal letter to one of the people below and choose the correct 'signing off' phrase.

   the bank manager   the editor of a newspaper

   your employer   the Head Teacher of your child's school

Suffixes (2)

Many longer words are made up of at least three distinct parts - a prefix, a root and a suffix. Adding a prefix or a suffix is often a quick way of changing the meaning of a root word.

e.g.   **un** *(prefix)* + **employ** *(root)* + **ment** *(suffix)* = **unemployment**

A **suffix** is a group of letters added to the end of a word. Sometimes the end of the root word is changed before the suffix is added. This often makes the word easier to say and it can also show the difference between two words with similar spellings.

A   -ly

The suffix ***-ly*** *comes from the Old English word* **lic***, which meant* **like***.*

The whole word is still used as an ending in words such as **childlike** *and* **warlike***.*

Some words change when ***-ly*** *is added, others stay the same. Write down the root word alongside each of the words below:*

1. slowly
2. faithfully
3. daily
4. shyly

5. truly
6. gaily
7. annually
8. likely

9. sincerely
10. fully
11. friendly
12. easily

B   -ish

The suffix ***-ish*** *also comes from Old English (originally* ***-isc****).*

When ***-ish*** *is added to a word it can do one of three things:*

1. *It can describe a person or thing's qualities (**e.g.** selfish)*
2. *It can say where someone comes from (**e.g.** English)*
3. *It can give a rough idea about someone or something (**e.g.** smallish; 2 o'clockish)*

Add some more words to each category:

1. selfish;
2. English;
3. smallish; 2 o'clockish;

C   Nationalities

1. *A person from China is* **Chinese***.*

    Think of some more nationalities with the same suffix.

2. *A person from Italy is* **Italian***.*

    Think of some more nationalities with the same suffix.

WRITING   1. *Write out a menu for a meal which includes your favourite ethnic dishes.*

2. *Write a short article which would encourage readers to try foreign travel or foreign food.*

Suffixes (3)

Many longer words are made up of at least three distinct parts - a prefix, a root and a suffix. Adding a prefix or a suffix is often a quick way of changing the meaning of a root word.

e.g. **un** *(prefix)* + **employ** *(root)* + **ment** *(suffix)* = **unemployment**

A **suffix** is a group of letters added to the end of a word. Sometimes the end of the root word is changed before the suffix is added. This often makes the word easier to say and it can also show the difference between two words with similar spellings.

A   Verbs into nouns

Many verbs can be changed into nouns by adding a suffix. Add one of the suffixes from the box to each of these verbs to give the person who does the job and the job they do. Change the ending of the verb where necessary. The first one is done for you.

verb	noun *(person)*	noun *(job)*
paint	painter	painting
decorate		
train		
build		
inspect		
supervise		
advertise		
drive		

or

er

ion

ment

ing

Add some more of your own.

B   Nouns into verbs

Each of these nouns is based on a verb. Write down the verb alongside each noun. The first one is done for you.

noun	verb	noun	verb
management	manage	decision	
equipment		exhibition	
excitement		explanation	
judgement		invitation	
enrolment		extension	
argument		admission	

Add some more of your own.

WRITING

Using as many words as you can which contain suffixes from the box above:

1. *Write a letter applying for a job advertised in the local newspaper.*
2. *Write to the Tourist Information Office asking about places to visit for a group of 10 or more on a day out.*

Suffixes (4)

Many longer words are made up of at least three distinct parts - a prefix, a root and a suffix. Adding a prefix or a suffix is often a quick way of changing the meaning of a root word.

    e.g.   **un** (*prefix*) + **employ** (*root*) + **ment** (*suffix*) = **unemployment**

A **suffix** is a group of letters added to the end of a word. Sometimes the end of the root word is changed before the suffix is added. This often makes the word easier to say and it can also show the difference between two words with similar spellings.

To double or not to double

It is always hard to decide when to double the last letter of a word before adding a suffix which begins with a vowel. It is almost impossible to make rules which are easy to apply because too many words don't follow them.

One way to decide what to do is to learn a key word as a mnemonic and apply it when you need to spell a word which works the same way. The exercises below give some ideas and examples of the most common spellings it is useful to know.

Remember: A standard dictionary will give you the correct spelling for a word and its usual suffixes.

A   *Single syllable words which end with 1 vowel and 1 consonant*

Double the last letter before adding a vowel suffix.   *Key word:* **fitting** (fit)

Add suffixes from the box to these words, doubling the last letter where necessary:

get	thin	rent	cut	act
run	wed	big	own	tip

er	ed	ing	est

B   *Words with 2 or more syllables which end with 1 vowel and 1 consonant*

With these words, the way that you say them is what matters. Say each word aloud.

If the stress is on the last syllable, double the last letter before adding a vowel suffix. *Key word:* **beginning** (begin)	If the stress is on the first syllable, do not double the last letter before adding a vowel suffix. *Key word:* **benefited** (benefit)

*Words which end in a vowel and **l** are different. They always double the last letter before adding a vowel suffix.*   *Key word:* **traveller** (*travel*)

Add suffixes from the box to these words, doubling the last letter where necessary:

target	occur	regret	limit	label
admit	budget	quarrel	prefer	

er	ed	ing	able

C   *What's the difference?*

The way these words are spelt tells you how to say them. Read each pair aloud, then put each word into a sentence which explains its meaning.

1.	dinner	diner	5.	tapped	taped
2.	filled	filed	6.	winning	wining
3.	hopped	hoped	7.	planned	planed
4.	bitter	biter	8.	slopping	sloping

                                                    Brown and Brown / Spelling Worksheets

Syllables

A **syllable** is a unit of sound which always contains a vowel (*a e i o u and sometimes y*).

❐ Words are made up of 1 or more syllables. *e.g. it* = 1 syllable; *in-for-ma-tion* = 4 syllables

❐ Breaking up a long word into separate syllables can be helpful in learning to spell it.

❐ It is best to try to look at words as groups of syllables or letter patterns, rather than single letters. You can then get to know whole groups of words which contain the same syllable or letter pattern.

A How many?

1. *How many syllables are there in these words:*

because   sincerely   interesting   different   exaggerate   every

2. *Give 3 or more words which contain the syllables underlined in these words:*

<u>be</u>fore   slowl<u>y</u>   <u>ex</u>pect   faith<u>ful</u>   bigg<u>est</u>

B Syllable poems (Haiku)

*The Japanese have invented very short poems called **haiku** (pron. high-koo). They always contain a set number of syllables and they are usually laid out in 3 lines.*

Each poem tries to capture a single moment from everyday life and make a little picture of it with just a few words - a bit like a snapshot. Haiku are now popular with writers all over the world because they are so short, they don't have to rhyme and they give the writer a framework for a poem.

Here are 3 examples. Read each poem aloud and write the number of syllables beside each line.

A bitter morning:
Sparrows sitting together
Without any necks.

The old rooster crows -
out of the mist come the rocks
and the twisted pine.

Gold, brown and red leaves
All twirling and scattering
As the children play.

WRITING   *Writing haiku is a good way for beginners to start writing poems.*

Use the pattern of syllables you have worked out from the poems above as the framework for a haiku of your own. Choose your own subject, or try one of these:

Spring   a hangover   an old man   Sunday morning

a black cat   a child   Summer in the city   snow

Using apostrophes

Punctuation helps a reader to understand exactly what a writer is saying. Everyone agrees that it is hard to make sense of a piece of writing which has no full stops and capital letters, but other punctuation marks can sometimes seem unnecessary or confusing. The one that gives most trouble is the apostrophe. It has 2 uses:

1. The word *apostrophe* comes from a Greek word which means 'a mark of omission'. When 2 or more words are shortened to make one word, an apostrophe replaces the missing letters *(e.g. I'll; weren't)*. In speech, we often shorten words. Using an apostrophe is a way of showing this in writing. Without it, a word can often mean something quite different. *(The exercises below are all based on this use of the apostrophe.)*

2. Unfortunately, in English, the apostrophe can also be used with an *s* to show possession:
   e.g. The Church of St. John is written as *St. John's Church*
   the kit of the footballers is written as *the footballers' kit*

   There is a lot of confusion between this and adding *-s* to a word to make it plural. It is now becoming very common to leave out the apostrophe rather than use it wrongly. This seems a sensible solution to the problem because, in this case, the apostrophe is rarely needed to make the meaning clear. What do you think?

A What's missing?

Put in the apostrophes missing from this letter. There are 14 altogether.

Dear Mrs. OConnor,

Im writing to let you know why Gillian didnt come to school today. She had a fall at six oclock yesterday. We havent been able to get through to you on the phone. Weve been worrying that shed broken her ankle, but the doctor says she hasnt, its just a sprain. He says that she cant walk on it for a week and we arent to let her go to school. Were hoping that shell be back by next Monday.

Yours sincerely,

Maureen MacDonald

Re-write the letter, writing out all the shortened words in full.

B What's the difference?

Explain the difference between these pairs of words:

1.	well	we'll	4.	ill	I'll	6.	wed	we'd
2.	hell	he'll	5.	its	it's	7.	shed	she'd
3.	shell	she'll						

WRITING

Write a letter complaining about faulty goods you have just received by mail order. Use some of the 'contractions' from the box, putting in the apostrophes first.

youve	wont	dont	Ive	arent	itll	theyre
wasnt	oughtnt	theres	wouldnt	wed	hadnt	

Vowel sounds and their spellings

Each of the 5 vowels *a e i o u* has 2 sounds - a long one and a short one.

This check list gives examples of the main ways in which each vowel sound can be spelt. It does not contain every spelling of every sound and some of the sounds may not apply to every region of the U.K.

Keep the list handy for quick reference and add extra sounds and spellings as you find them.

Sound	Spelling	Example	Sound	Spelling	Example
Short *a*	a	at	Long *a*	a	age
	au	laugh *(North)*		ay	day
				ai	rain
				aigh	straight
				ea	great
				ei	veil
				eigh	weigh
				ey	they
Short *e*	e	end	Long *e*	e	me
	ea	head		ee	feet
	a	any		ea	seat
	ai	said		ei	receipt
	ie	friend		eo	people
				i	police
				ie	niece
Short *i*	i	it	Long *i*	i	ice
	ui	build		ie	lie
	y	gym		igh	high
				ei	either
				eigh	height
				uy	buy
				y	try
				ye	goodbye
Short *o*	o	on	Long *o*	o	old
	ough	cough		oa	goal
	a	was		oe	toe
	au	because		ou	soul
				ough	though
				ow	own
Short *u*	u	up	Long *u*	u	use
	o	other		ue	due
	oe	does		eau	beauty
	oo	blood		eu	neutral
	ou	enough		ew	new
				iew	view
				ou	you

What is English?

English is a mixture of languages brought to the British Isles by settlers and invaders over many centuries. Celts came from France and the Netherlands in 400 BC, followed by the Romans. Angles, Saxons and Jutes came next from Denmark, Germany and Holland. Then there were the Vikings from Norway and Denmark; and last of all, in 1066, William the Conqueror brought French into English in a big way. Since then, Britain's history of exploration and empire-building in other countries and the huge increase in world trade, travel and communications over the last century have meant that thousands of foreign words have been absorbed into the language and are an accepted part of everyday speech.

English people are well-known for their inability to speak foreign languages, yet their own language is full of words from practically every country in the world. "It's all Greek to me," they say, quoting Shakespeare. "or double Dutch." They don't realise how many Greek or Dutch words they use every day of their lives.

A   Good Old English

The words listed below are spelt as they were in Old English. They can all be found in the piece above. Tick those which have changed their spelling. Write down the modern spelling alongside the others. Use a standard dictionary to help, if you like.

of	bi	and	ofer	fram	laetest
thenne	worold	thaet	thusend	word	daeg

B   Up-to-date English

Use a standard dictionary to find the origin of these words:

anorak	boss	caravan	chocolate	curry	job
knife	pal	pizza	plastic	quiz	silk	television

C   What's your word ?

There are many different dialects in English and different ways of saying the same thing, depending on where people live.

1.   Think of as many phrases as you can for

- saying 'Hello'
- saying 'Goodbye'
- saying 'Thanks'
- saying something is very good
- saying something is very bad

2.   Make a list of words and phrases which are only used in your locality.

WRITING   a.   *Write a few sentences about the area where you live, spelling the words exactly as you would say them in your own accent.*

b.   *Rewrite your sentences in standard English spelling so that a reader from another part of the country could understand them.*

What's in your name?

You can use your name to help you to think about spelling. There are some ideas on this sheet and you can add others yourself.

Print your name in this box, then do the exercises below.

A Beginnings

1. **a.** Write down 2 other first names which begin with the same sound as yours.

    b. Write down 2 other surnames which begin with the same sound as yours.

send	after	bike	taxi	zoo	on	sheet	dear	ice
garage	cost	joke	mail	know	post	write	hand	
was	fill	eat	every	red	early	vet	little	yet

2. **a.** Pick out any words from the box above which begin with the same sound as your first name. Add 2 more words of your own.

    b. Pick out any words from the box above which begin with the same sound as your surname. Add 2 more words of your own.

B Endings
*Repeat Section A , looking at words which **end** with the same sound as your first name and your surname.*

C Syllables

a. How many syllables are there in your first name? Write down 2 other first names with the same number of syllables as yours.

b. How many syllables are there in your surname? Write down 2 other surnames with the same number of syllables as yours.

D What does it mean?

a. Does your first name have a special meaning? *e.g.* *Margaret* means *pearl* or *daisy*. Look up your name in a dictionary of first names.

b. *Originally people in Britain had only one name, such as John or Peter. Later, surnames were added to identify people who had the same first name. The simplest form of surname said whose son the person was:*

e.g. John, son of *Peter*, became *John Peterson*

Hamish, son of *Arthur*, became *Hamish MacArthur*

People were also named after the place where they lived, or their job, or how they looked and in many other ways.

e.g. Redhead; Lightfoot; Brown; Carpenter; Bridge; Field

Where does your surname come from? Look it up in a dictionary of surnames.

What's in your address?

You can use your address to help you to think about spelling. There are some ideas on this sheet and you can add others yourself.

Print your address and postcode in the box, then do the exercises.

1. Write down all the words you know for the streets where people live.
   e.g. street; road

2. Write down all the words you know for the buildings in which people live.
   e.g. house; castle

3. How many syllables are there in your address?

4. Make a list of words which have the same spelling patterns and sounds as some of those in your address (*e.g. Glasgow - window, know, show, slow*)

5. *Streets are often named after famous people, places, events, flowers, birds etc.*
   e.g. Station Road; Trafalgar Square; Beech Lane
   What other street names could be in a group with yours?

6. *The names of towns, cities and villages often contain parts which are found in many others. These parts are often old words with a special meaning.*
   e.g. Birmingham; Aberystwyth; Stalybridge; Ballycastle; Warwick; Southampton; Dundee
   a. Look up the underlined parts of the places in the example above in a Dictionary of Place-names to find their original meaning.
   b. Look up your town in a Dictionary of Place-names to find out what the name means.
   c. Look on a map for other place-names which are like yours.

7. Name the counties which are next to the one you live in. If you live in a city, which counties are nearest to you?

8. Except in London, most postcodes start with the first letter and often one other from the name of a town or city. What do the first 1 or 2 letters of your postcode stand for?

WRITING   *Here are some interesting street and place names. Choose 4 of them and write down your own short explanation of the origin of each name.*

Bythesea Road	Breadmarket Street	Foundry Lane
Heavitree	Hangingstone Road	Balloon Street
Hot Bath Street	Ragged Appleshaw	Fishguard
Cowpen Road	Gas Street	Rope Walk

Brown and Brown / Spelling Worksheets

Terms used in *Spelling Worksheets*

It is quicker and easier to learn the accepted terms for describing the English language and its spelling. Many of them come from Latin and Greek, as do so many technical words, and they manage to say in one word what would otherwise take many words.

The terms on this sheet are those used in *Spelling Worksheets*. A standard dictionary will give information on terms which are not included here.

Apostrophe	A punctuation mark ' which is used to show that letters are missing from a word *(e.g. wasn't, it's)* or to show possession *(e.g. Keeper's Cottage)*.
Consonant	20 letters of the alphabet are consonants: *b c d f g h j k l m n p q r s t v w x z*. *y* can be a consonant or a vowel.
Homonym	Homonyms are words which are spelt the same way but have different meanings and, sometimes, different pronunciations *(e.g. row - to row a boat; row - an argument)*.
Homophone	Homophones are words which are spelt differently and have different meanings, but sound the same *(e.g. road and rode)*.
Language	**(Origin**: Latin *lingua* = tongue) The most common language for humans is the system of communication which uses spoken sounds and written symbols. Compare it with *body language, animal language, the language of love*.
Mnemonic	Mnemonics are memory aids or tricks which can help us remember spellings.
Noun	One of the words, known as parts of speech, which describe the kinds of words which make up language. A noun gives a name to a person, place, thing or feeling *(e.g. woman, Africa, bottle, anger)*. Other parts of speech are: *pronoun, adjective, verb, adverb, preposition, conjunction, interjection*.
Plural	A plural word describes more than one of anything. It usually ends in **s**. Compare it with *singular*.
Prefix	A group of letters added to the beginning of a word *(e.g. pre-, dis-, extra-)*.
Proof reading	Re-reading and checking any piece of writing. A proof is a rough printed copy of a piece of professional writing which is read and corrected before publishing.
Punctuation	A system of marks which divides up writing to make the meaning clear. Punctuation marks are *(see above for the apostrophe)*: full stop **.** comma **,** question mark **?** exclamation mark **!** quotation marks **" "** or **' '** *always used in pairs* colon **:** semi-colon **;** dash or hyphen **-** brackets **( )**
Root	The part of a longer word which contains the basic meaning *(e.g. faith is the root of unfaithful)*.
Spelling pattern	A group of letters often seen together in words *(e.g. str-, -ble, ea, th)*.
Suffix	A group of letters added to the end of a word *(e.g. -ing, -ment, -ful)*.
Syllable	A syllable is a unit of sound which always contains a vowel *(e.g. im port ant has 3 syllables)*
Verb	A verb is a part of speech which describes an action of any kind *(e.g. eat, run, feel, think)*. See **Noun** above for the names of the other parts of speech.
Vowel	5 letters of the alphabet are vowels: *a e i o u*. The letter *y* is sometimes a vowel and sometimes a consonant.

Useful reference books

The books in this list are of 2 kinds. The dictionaries will be of help to you while you are doing the worksheets. The general books on spelling will provide extra practice or information on particular spelling points.

Note: Your local public library will either have or be able to get any of these books for you. If you do not already belong to a library, **join one now**. The U.K. has the best library service in the world. Make sure you use it.

Dictionaries

Standard

Collins English Dictionary *3rd revised edition 1991*

Collins Thesaurus (A-Z format) *Revised edition 1992*

*This dictionary is, in our opinion, by far the best standard dictionary (**i.e.** one which contains full details about a word, its meaning and its origin). It also includes information which would otherwise only be found in an encyclopaedia - names of famous people and places, for example. The Thesaurus is arranged in alphabetical order, like a dictionary, which makes it much easier to use than most others. It is available separately or in a combined edition with the dictionary.*

Spelling

Cassell's Spelling Dictionary by L.B. and D. Firnberg *Cassell New 2nd Revised Edition 1993*

Spell it Yourself by G.T. Hawker *O.U.P. 2nd Revised Edition 1992*

Special interest

Brewer's Dictionary of Phrase and Fable *Cassell 2nd Revised Edition 1981*

Brewer's 20th Century Dictionary of Phrase and Fable *Cassell 1991*

The Concise Oxford Dictionary of English Place-names   ed. Eilert Ekwall
O.U.P. 4th Edition 1977

The Oxford Dictionary of English Christian Names by E.G. Withycombe
O.U. P. 3rd revised edition 1977

A Dictionary of British Surnames by P.H. Reaney
Routledge & Kegan Paul 3rd revised edition 1991

General books on Spelling

A Guide to Better Spelling by Angela Burt *Stanley Thornes 1982*

A Speller's Companion by Margaret Brown *Brown and Brown 2nd Edition 1990*

Spelling It Out by Rhiannedd Pratley *BBC Books 1988*

Spelling Matters by Bernard R. Sadler *Edward Arnold 1982 (o/p)*